The Interna

MW00788192

ARTS & CRAFTS PATTERNS & DESIGNS
BY
PHOEBE ANN ERB

Stemmer
House
Publishers

Copyright © 2004 by Phoebe Erb Gallagher
All rights reserved

All individual designs in this book may be used in any manner without permission. However, no grouping of 15 or more designs in a single collection for commercial purposes, and no part of the text, may be used or reproduced in any manner whatsoever, electronic or mechanical, including xerography, microfilm, Internet, recording and photocopying, without written permission, except in the case of brief quotations in critical articles and reviews. The book may not be reproduced as a whole, or in substantial part, without permission in writing from the publishers.

Inquiries should be directed to
Stemmer House Publishers
4 White Brook Road
Gilsum, NH 03448
U.S.A.

Printed and bound in the United States of America

A Barbara Holdridge book

First Edition

Colophon
Designed by Barbara Holdridge
Composed in Times with P22 Arts & Crafts display,
  originally designed by Dard Hunter for Roycraft Press
Printed on 75-pound Williamsburg Return Card paper and bound by
  United Graphics, Inc., Mattoon, Illinois

Phoebe Ann Erb is the author of four previous titles in the extensive International Design Library® series, listed on the back cover: *Floral Designs from Traditional Printed Handkerchiefs, Medieval Floral Designs, William Morris Patterns & Designs* and *Art Deco Patterns & Designs.* A textile designer, she also teaches textile print design, collects printed textiles and creates artist books.

Author's Note: The images on the following pages were culled from books, as well as from journals, magazines and art manuals of the era, including *The Studio, School Arts Magazine* and *The House Beautiful,* among others. The drawings represent details from textiles, furnishings, ceramics, advertising and book graphics. Most of the drawings have been enlarged or reduced for the purposes of this book. Identification includes source, designer and country of origin, if known, and exact or approximate dates.

EMBROIDERED CUSHION.
ANN MACBETH. GLASGOW. 1901

Introduction

THE ARTS AND CRAFTS MOVEMENT FLOURISHED APPROXIMATELY between 1880 and 1920. It began in England as a reaction both to the social upheavals of the Industrial Revolution and to the inferior quality of machine-made products. Critics deplored the "abominable" over-decoration and "shoddy" craftsmanship of the household goods showcased at the Great Exhibition of 1851.

Art historian John Ruskin sowed the seeds of the Arts and Crafts Movement. Workers in dehumanized factories had become "mere cogs in the wheels of machinery," turning out a glut of standardized products that possessed no true sense of design. Ruskin believed that only by returning to hand production could satisfaction in work be restored and the ills of society corrected.

William Morris, disciple of Ruskin, fathered the movement. Evoking the craft guilds of the Middle Ages, he founded Morris & Company in 1875, and later, Kelmscott Press. Morris fashioned his chintzes and wallpapers, filled with birds and flowers, after Gothic styles that he found simple and clear—in contrast to the design confusion of his own Victorian era. He avoided the garish chemical dyes of the day and made his own vegetable dyes in subdued greens, terra cotta, browns and yellows.

Morris' example spurred other artisans to establish cooperative workshops that valued good working environment and craftsmanship as much as production: Ernest W. Gimson in furniture, William de Morgan in pottery, T. J. Cobden-Sanderson in bookbinding, C. F. Voysey in textiles and wallpaper. Replete with beautifully drawn birds and animals, Voysey's designs epitomized the look of English Arts and Crafts.

Architect C. R. Ashbee's Guild of Handicrafts included cabinet-makers, metalworkers, enamelers and book printers. In Scotland, Charles Rennie Mackintosh and Margaret MacDonald in architecture, furnishings and textiles led the way with the lean "Glasgow Style." Century Guild, organized by A. H. Mackmurdo, worked with manufacturers to improve mass-produced goods.

During the 1880s, numerous societies for the promotion of handicrafts were founded. The Arts and Crafts Exhibition Society, led by Walter Crane, prolific illustrator of books and wallpapers, preached the equality of the applied and fine arts and stressed that well-made objects for average people would improve their lives.

Similar ideas were promoted in journals such as *Hobby Horse* and *The Studio,* which sponsored annual design competitions as well.

The ideals of the English Arts and Crafts movement spread to other industrialized European countries, and to the United States, where Ruskin and Morris were widely read. The prototypes of many Societies of Arts and Crafts in the United States were founded in Boston and Chicago in 1897. The societies held lectures and classes and promoted public art education. They encouraged individual creativity and artistic experimentation, provided workspace and held exhibitions for members.

Japanese art—all the rage in the late nineteenth century, with its pure color, bold lines, flattened shapes and emphasis on composition rather than naturalistic drawing—also had a crucial influence on the American Arts and Crafts aesthetics.

Dozens of artist-handicraft communities engaged in furniture-making, bookbinding and art pottery–Pauline Pottery in Wisconsin and Newcomb Pottery in New Orleans, for example–sprang up across North America. The best known were Elbert Hubbard's Roycroft Shops and Press (inspired by Morris' Kelmscott Press), established in 1895 and Gustav Stickley's Craftsman enterprises, begun in 1901.

Roycroft Shops, in upstate New York, made simply styled wooden furniture and household articles, such as wrought iron candlesticks and copperware. Book titles from Roycroft ranged from *Nature* by Emerson to *Woman's Work* by Alice Hubbard, and sold in huge quantities. Hubbard, with his "made with our head, hand and heart" sales pitch, proved to be a savvy entrepreneur. By 1906, hundreds of people worked in his community to meet the demand for "made-to-order" Roycroft products.

Gustav Stickley's Craftsman Workshops in Syracuse, New York combined hand-craftsmanship with machine work. Stickley furniture, with its plain, straight lines, woodgrain surfaces and natural colors, came to represent the no-nonsense American Arts and Crafts look.

Stickley published *The Craftsman*, a monthly Arts and Crafts journal. Subjects ranged from healing the "insane" through work, growing corn and basket-weaving, to studying the relationship of women and housework. He touted the "simple life": a return to nature, hearth and home as moral ideals. He published do-it-yourself architectural plans and costs for modest houses. Consequently, by 1910 "Craftsman bungalows," as these houses became known, were everywhere. Craftsman houses were designed to make the most of sunshine, air and the view. They were usually made of timber or cement, often with large porches, ideally set on a woodsy lot. Interiors had built-in features, such as bookcases of oak and other hardwoods. Wood wainscoting, tiled and hand-stenciled walls (patterns for householders appeared in home magazines) in organic colors accented the down-to-earth nature of the house.

Bungalows were especially suited to California, with its wholesome weather and plentiful oak, redwood and pine. There, acclaimed architects Charles and Henry Greene developed the "Ultimate Bungalow," complete with custom furnishings and interior details–door knobs, fireplace tools, carpets, lead glass and so forth–for wealthy clients.

The Arts and Crafts Movement, while aiming to bring beauty into everyone's lives, in the end introduced it mainly to the affluent. Critics pointed out that the "visible imperfections" of hand-made goods were signs of snobbery and "conspicuous consumption." The Movement's prized simplicity was actually labor-intensive, and therefore beyond the means of most.

Technology and new materials were developing rapidly in the early twentieth century. In the Midwest, the work of Frank Lloyd Wright was a harbinger of things to come. His respect for natural materials, expert craftsmanship, simplicity and unity of design were rooted in the Arts and Crafts Movement. However, he recognized that beauty for all lay in machine production. In a 1901 speech at the Chicago Society of Arts and Crafts, Wright maintained: "The machine, by its wonderful cutting, shaping, smoothing and repetitive capacity, has made it possible to so use it without waste that the poor as well as the rich may enjoy today beautiful surface treatments of clean, strong forms."

By 1920, the Arts and Crafts ethos of hand-craftsmanship and natural materials had completely given way to modernist thinking that embraced machines and industrial materials. Le Corbusier's house, a "machine for living," replaced the cozy Craftsman hearth and home. Nevertheless, a current California quarterly, *American Bungalow*, is dedicated to preserving and restoring this uniquely American dwelling.

There is also lively interest among collectors and museums in Arts and Crafts objects and in the Movement's influence on modern design. In the fall of 2004, the exhibition, "The Course of Invention: The Arts and Crafts Movement in Europe and America: Design for the Modern World, 1880-1920," opened at the Los Angeles County Museum, with another exhibit, "International Arts and Crafts," displayed at the V&A Museum, London, in the spring of 2005.   P.A.E.
Dedicated to
All who use this book

**Selected
Bibliography**

Clark, Robert Judson, Editor. *Arts & Crafts Movement in America: 1876–1916.* Princeton: Princeton University Press, 1992

Kaplan, Wendy. *The Arts & Crafts Movement in Europe and America: Design for the Modern World.* New York and London: Thames and Hudson in association with the Los Angeles County Museum of Art, 2004

Lambourne, Lionel. *Utopian Craftsman: The Arts & Crafts Movement from the Cotswolds to Chicago.* Salt Lake City: Peregrine Smith, Inc., 1980

Livingston, Karen and Perry, Linda (Eds.). *International Arts and Crafts.* London: V&A Publications, 2005

Naylor, Gillian. *The Arts & Crafts Movement: A Study of its Sources, Ideals, & Influence on Design Theory.* Cambridge, Massachusetts: The MIT Press, 1971

Parry, Linda. *William Morris and the Arts & Crafts Movement.* New York: Portland House, 1989

Front cover Cover detail. Opera libretto, "Iris" by Luigi Illica. Music by Pietro Mascagni. G. Ricordi & Co. Milan, 1898

Back cover *The Craftsman*, cover. Gustav Stickley, editor and publisher. New York, March 1916

Title Page "Fairyland" wallpaper. C.F.A.Voysey for Essex & Co. England, 1896

Page 2 Embroidered cushion. Ann Macbeth. Glasgow, 1901

Page 3 *Top right:* Rose stencil. Charles Rennie Mackintosh. Glasgow, 1900 *Lower right:* Ladderback chair. Charles Rennie Mackintosh. Glasgow, 1903

Page 4 *Top:* Woodblock design. *The House Beautiful.* U.S., August 1910 *Lower right:* Cover detail. The Fra. Dard Hunter, for Roycroft Printing Shop. East Aurora, N.Y., May 1915

Page 5 *Dedication:* Stationery box lid. George Auriol. France, c. 1900 *Lower:* Book cover detail. Entry, *The Studio* prize competition. London, 1893

Page 6 Top left: Book cover detail. Dard Hunter, for Roycroft Printing Shop. East Aurora, N.Y., 1908

Plates

1. *Top left:* Cover illustration, *School Arts Magazine.* Davis Press, Worcester, MA, June 1916 *Top center and right:* Stencil designs from Davis Press, Worcester, MA., 1907 *Lower:* Poster illustration. George Bell & Sons, Ltd., London. 1895

2. *Top:* Gold and enamel border. John Lunkenhein, for Keramic Studio. Syracuse, N.Y., 1923 *Lower:* Cover illustration, *The Craftsman.* Gustav Stickley, editor and publisher. New York, October 1914

3. *Top:* Magazine graphic from *Art et Décoration.* Paris, June 1899 *Center:* Tooled leather book cover. André Mare. France, c. 1914 *Lower:* Stenciled border from *School Arts Magazine.* Davis Press, Worcester, MA., 1909

4. *Top:* Illustration. Arthur Wesley Dow, from *Composition: A Series of Exercises in Art Structure for the Use of Students and Teachers.* Doubleday & Co. New York, 1913 *Lower:* Embroidery design. M. P. Verneul. France, 1897

5. "Isis" wallpaper design. F. A. Voysey for Jeffrey & Co. England, c. 1895

6. *Top & left:* Examples of picture composition. Arthur Wesley Dow, from *Composition: A Series of Exercises in Art Structure for the Use of Students and Teachers.* Doubleday & Co. New York, 1913 *Lower right:* Stationery box lid. France, c. 1900

7. *Top:* Stationery box lid. France, c. 1900 *Lower three:* Examples of picture composition. Arthur Wesley Dow, from *Composition: A Series of Exercises in Art Structure for the Use of Students and Teachers.* Doubleday & Co., New York, 1913

8. *Top:* Wallpaper. C. F. A. Voysey, for Jeffrey & Co. England, c.1901 *Left:* Poster. Maurice Prendergast, for Joseph Knight Company Publishers. Boston, MA.,1895 *Top right:* Book cover detail. Entry, *The Studio* prize competition. London, 1896 *Lower right:* "Peacock" wallpaper detail. V. F. A. Voysey, for Jeffrey & Co. England, 1890s

9. *Top left:* Greeting card graphic from *School Arts Book.* Davis Press. Worcester, MA.,1909 *Top right:* Stained glass. John C. Hall for Scottish Guild of Handicraft, Ltd., 1906 *Center:* Book cover detail. T. J. Cobden-Sanderson, for Doves Press. London, 1885 *Right:* Stained glass. William Morris & Co. London, c.1906 *Lower:* Fireplace decoration. Talvin Morris. England,1897

10. *Top:* Ceramic plate. Blanche Lazzell. U. S., 1907 *Center & lower:* Tile designs from *School Arts Magazine.* Davis Press. Worcester, MA. June 1916

11. *Top left:* Cloisonné pot. Grueby Pottery. Boston, MA., c.1897 *Top center:* Cut velvet floral detail. A. H. Mackmurdo. England, c.1880s *Top right:* Glass vase. Heinrich Wollman for Orrefors Glass. Sweden, 1916. *Lower:* Plate borders. Dedham Pottery. Dedham, MA., c. 1914

12. *Top left:* Letter paper detail. George Auriol. France, 1900 *Top right:* Stencil design from *School Arts Book.* Davis Press, Worcester, MA., 1909 *Center:* "The Sleeping Beauty." wallpaper detail. Walter Crane, for Jeffrey & Co. England, 1879

13. *Top:* Illustration. Walter Crane. *Flora's Feast, A Masque of Flowers.* Cassel & Co. Ltd., London, 1899 *Lower:* Stencil border, *School Arts Book.* Davis Press, Worcester , MA., 1909

14. Tooled leather book cover. André Mare. France, 1914

15. *Top:* Embroidered cushion. Ann Macbeth. Glasgow, 1906 *Lower:* Embroidered panel. Ann Macbeth. Glasgow, 1906

16. *Top left:* Advertisement for Faience tableware. France, 1899 *Lower left:* Stencil design. Walter Crane, from *Line and Form.* George Bell & Sons. London, 1900 *Right:* Book cover detail. Entry, *The Studio* prize competition. London, 1893

17. Tooled leather book cover. William Launder. U. S., 1902 *Right:* Tailpieces. Wenzel Oswald. Austria, 1914 *Lower:* Tailpiece. Herbert P. Horne for *Hobby Horse.* London, 1886

18. Floral borders. Entries, *The Studio* prize competition. London, 1896

19. *Top left:* Illustration. Arthur Wesley Dow, from *Composition: A Series of Exercises in Art Structure for the Use of Students and Teachers.* Doubleday & Co. New York, 1913 *Top right & lower:* Embroidery designs. France, October 1899

20. Stencil wallpaper frieze. Rex Silver, for John Line & Sons, Ltd. England, c.1905

21. Stencil wallpaper frieze. Rex Silver, for John Line & Sons, Ltd. England, c.1905

22. *Top:* "Fig & Olive" textile design. C. F. A. Voysey for Jeffrey & Co. England, 1897 *Lower left:* Ceramic border design. Keramic Studio. Syracuse, 1914 *Lower right:* Tailpiece, *Knight Errant.* Boston, MA., 1892

23. *Top:* Cover illustration. *The International Studio, An Illustrated Monthly Magazine of Fine and Applied Arts.* New York, 1901 *Lower left:* Design for lectern inlay. Ernest W. Gimson. London, 1906 *Lower right:* Book cover. Dard Hunter, for Roycroft Press. East Aurora, N.Y., 1905

24. *Left:* Wallpaper detail. England, c.1906 *Right:* Stained glass window. Alex Gascoyne for George F. Gascoyne & Sons. London, 1906 *Lower:* Advertisement graphic, *The House Beautiful.* Chicago, June 1905

25. Illustrations. Walter Crane, from *Line and Form.* George Bell & Sons, London, Ltd., 1900

26. *Top:* Bookbinding case detail. R. P. Cossop, for J.M. Dent & Sons, Ltd. England, c. 1914 *Left & center:* Spring motifs, *School Arts Magazine.* Davis Press. Worcester, MA., April 1917 *Center right:* Title-page graphic by Blasius Busay. Arts and Crafts School. Budapest, 1914 *Lower left:* Book cover graphic. T. J. Cobden-Sanderson for Doves Press. London, 1893 *Lower right:* Tailpiece, *Knight Errant.* Boston, MA., July 1892

27. *Top:* Calendar graphic, *School Arts Book.* Davis Press, Worcester, MA., 1909 *Lower:* "The Braunton" wallpaper. Harry Napper, for Alexander Rottman & Co. England, 1902

28. *Top:* Stencil motif. Walter Crane, from *Line and Form.* George Bell & Sons. London, 1900 *Lower:* Covered jar. Pauline Jacobus, for Pauline Pottery. Edgerton, WI., c. 1902

29. *Top left:* Stencil motif. Walter Crane, from *Line and Form,* George Bell & Sons. London, 1900. *Top right:* Wallpaper design. Pictured in *The House Beautiful.* Chicago, May 1903 *Left:* Vase. Mary G. Sheerer, for Newcomb College Pottery. New Orleans, c.1895 *Lower:* Toiletware. Léon V. Salon, for Mintons, Ltd. England, 1906

30. *Top:* Tailpiece, *Hobby Horse.* Herbert P. Horne. England, 1882 *Center:* Ceramic tile. Maud M. Mason for Keramic Studio. Syracuse, N.Y., 1916

31. Book cover illustration. Entry, *The Studio* prize competition. London, 1893

32. *Top:* Wilton carpet border. Liberty & Co., Ltd. London, 1906 *Center:* Embossed silver tray. C. R. Ashbee, for the Guild of Handicraft. England, 1896-97

33. *Left:* Ceramic tiles. William de Morgan. England, c.1900 *Right:* Ceramic tiles. William de Morgan. England, c.1900

34. "The Spies" appliqué panel. Godfrey Blount, for Haslemere Peasant Industries. England, c. 1900

35. *Top left:* Home library advertisement graphic from *The House Beautiful.* Chicago, May 1904 *Top right:* "Burcot" wallpaper. C. K. Lennox, for C. Knowles & Co. Ltd. England, 1906 *Lower left:* Table mat embroidery. Ann Macbeth. Glasgow, 1906 *Lower right:* Pyrography appliqué. Thayer & Chandler. U.S.,1904

36. Stenciled book cover. Entry, *The Studio* prize competition. London, 1896

37. *Top left & right:* Ceramics decoration. Kathryn E. Cherry, for Keramic Studio. Syracuse, 1915-1917 *Center:* China decoration. Nellie Hagan, for Keramic Studio. Syracuse, 1922 *Lower:* Border design. John Luckenhein, for Keramic Studio. Syracuse, 1923

38. *Left:* Cover illustration. *The Craftsman.* Gustav Stickley, publisher and editor. New York, April 1914 *Right:* Ceramics decoration. Kathryn E. Cherry, for Keramic Studio. Syracuse, 1917

39. *Top & lower left:* Ceramics decoration. Kathryn E. Cherry, for Keramic Studio. Syracuse, 1917 *Top right:* Book cover detail. Entry, *The Studio* prize competition. London, 1894 *Lower right:* Ladderback Chair. C.R. Mackintosh. Glasgow, 1903

40. "The Bay Leaf" wallpaper and frieze design. Herbert Horne, for Jeffrey & Co. England, c. 1882

41. *Top:* Tailpiece from *The Craftsman.* Gustav Stickley, publisher and editor. New York, 1916 *Center:* Book cover. Samuel Warner, for Roycroft Printing Shop. East Aurora, N.Y., 1901 *Lower:* Stencil motifs from *School Arts Magazine.* Davis Publishing, Worcester, MA., 1907

42. *Top left & right:* Motif variations. Albert W. Hechman, for Keramic Studio. Syracuse, 1914. *Center left:* Textile design. England, 1909 *Center:* Book cover detail. Thomas Bird Mosher. England, 1900. *Right:* Stenciled canvas chairback. Glasgow, 1902 *Lower left:* Ad graphic for Liberty Glass. Toledo, OH., 1905

2

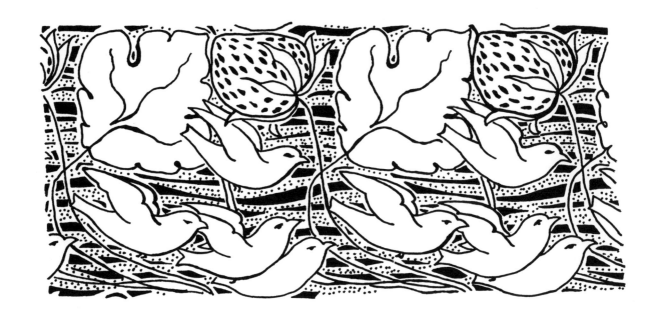

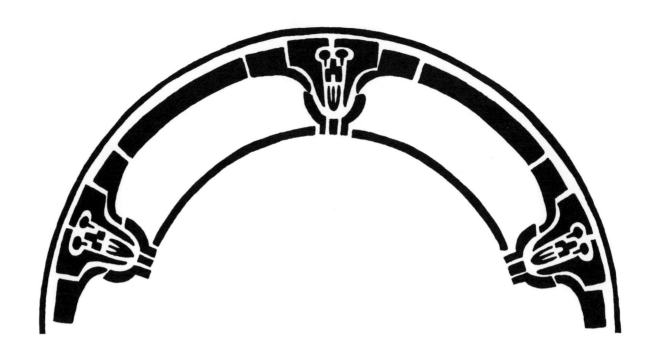

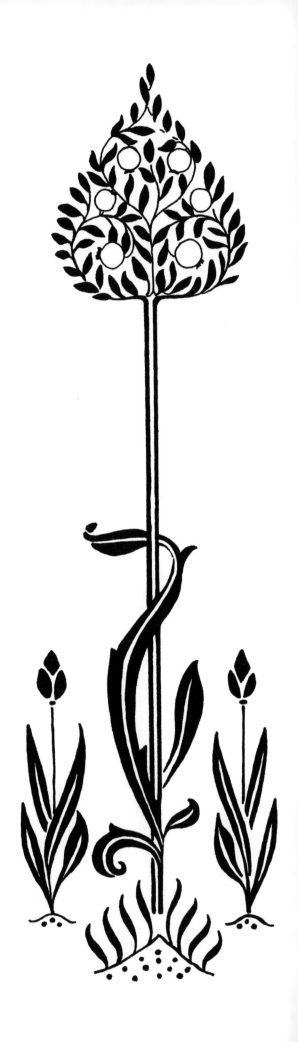

NATVRE

EMERSON

GATHER
ye
ROSEBUDS

24

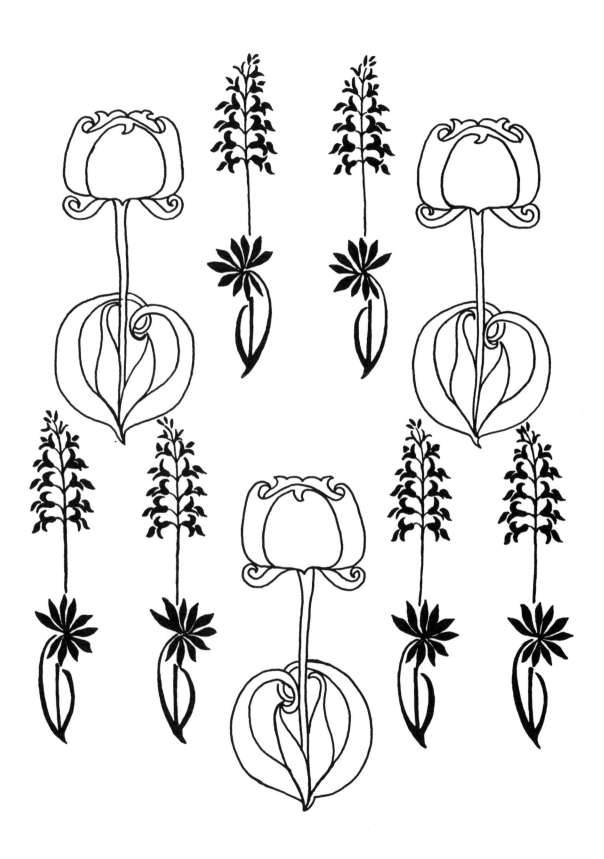

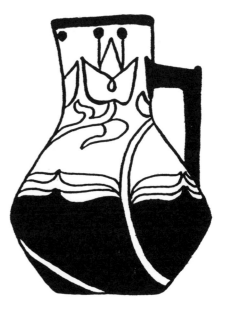

34

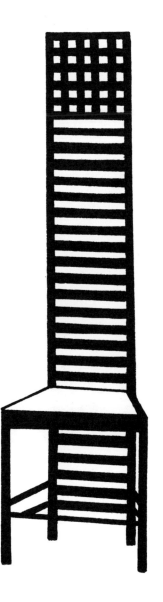

39

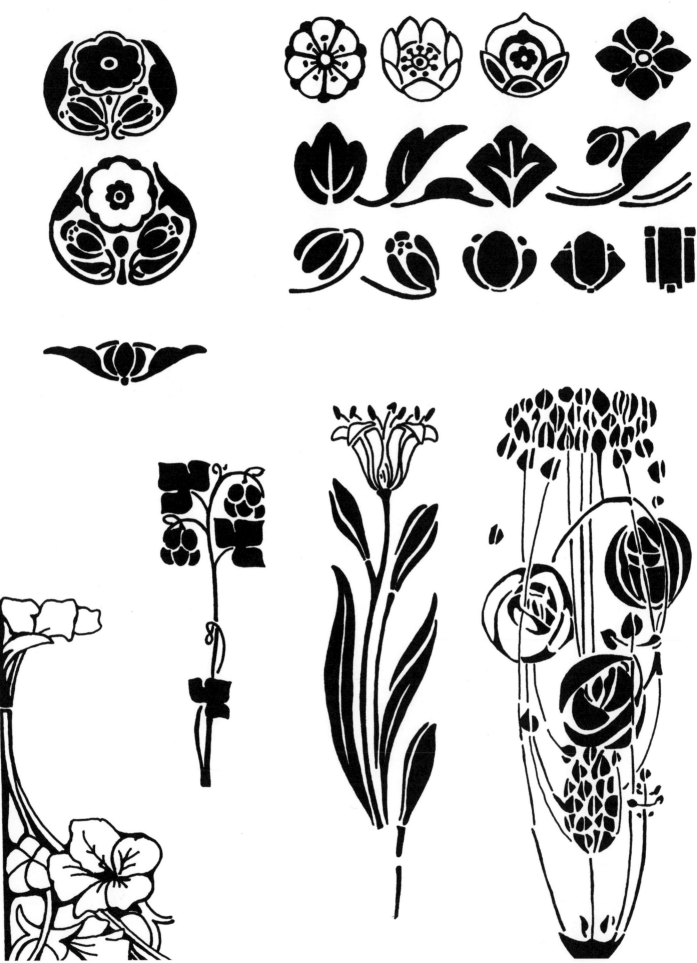